T0019788

NO DOCUMENT

NO DOCUMENT
Anwen Crawford

TRANSIT
BOOKS

Published by Transit Books
2301 Telegraph Avenue, Oakland, California 94612
www.transitbooks.org

First published in Australia by Giramondo Publishing, 2021
© Anwen Crawford 2021

ISBN: 978-1-945492-61-7 (paperback) | 978-1-945492-63-1 (ebook)
LIBRARY OF CONGRESS CONTROL NUMBER: 2022930467

DESIGN & TYPESETTING
Justin Carder

DISTRIBUTED BY
Consortium Book Sales & Distribution
(800) 283-3572 | cbsd.com

Printed in the United States of America

9 8 7 6 5 4 3 2 1

 This project is supported in part by an award from the National
Endowment for the Arts.

You could say an event in history is over, the way a book is slapped shut when it is done. But where is the marker?

Fanny Howe

Georges Franju's documentary *Le Sang des Bêtes* begins with the slaughter of a white horse.

Or so I had remembered.

A man leads a horse by its bridle through the gates of an abattoir. The horse and the man stand together in the courtyard of the abattoir.

The pressure applied by the man as he places a captive bolt gun to the head of the horse appears gentle, as the touch of one's lips upon the face of a person to whom you are saying goodbye, and perhaps for a long time.

I was young for a long time. Nobody died. Perhaps I wanted to die, or thought that I did, but that is not the same.

As the man drives the bolt through the brain of the white horse its legs buckle instantaneously. It seems to bounce from the pavement into the air before crashing onto its flank.

To be stunned.

The word comes from *thunder*.

What I really mean is that no death had overturned me.

During the second semester of my first year at art school you bring a sequence of black-and-white photographs to class.

Our first year at art school. Some years after your death I find a notebook in which you have written MY WORK—in blunt pencil, as you always wrote—and then crossed out the MY for OUR. Our work.

I think of the way in which the horse turns its head in order to face the man who holds the captive bolt gun.

Or the texture of the back of your hands and the ways in which you moved them.

The photographs you bring into class show you kneeling at night on a pavement, digging through the concrete till it cracks, and then planting a sapling in the new wound.

Sous les pavés, la plage!

That's when I know we have to be friends.

Your white skin tanned; your brown panelled nylon zip-up jacket; the rat's tail of red hair that ran below your shoulders, till you cut it off; your hands

Or does the man who holds the gun pull upon the horse's bridle?

On my laptop I watch a contemporary drama set in London, featuring two women who are asylum seekers from Syria. Only, it transpires that the women are not Syrian, they are Iraqi, and this makes them economic migrants, not asylum seekers, and so they are taken into detention. At the detention centre, a guard observes to a cop: *It's a lot like a slaughterhouse. You need to calm the animals.*

The first thing we make is a fence / on Wangal country, unrolling the wire mesh across the width of the gallery.

For an instant, with its forelegs drawn into the air, the stunned horse recalls a statuary horse on a carousel.

The borders of present-day Iraq have existed only since 1920, when the Treaty of Sèvres allowed the victorious Allied Powers of the First World War to partition the Ottoman Empire. The Treaty of Sèvres was signed at the Sèvres national porcelain manufactory, in the suburbs of Paris.

Aux porte de Paris, reads the opening caption of *Le Sang des Bêtes*: At the gates of Paris.

At each end we staple-gun the mesh to the walls.

August Macke, the German painter, was killed by French artillery fire on 26 September 1914, during the second month of the First World War. He was twenty-seven. His compatriot and fellow artist, Franz Marc, who had also been drafted, did not learn of August's death for nearly a month. *Oh dearest*, Marc wrote to his wife Maria, on 23 October, *the naked fact will not enter my head.*

I think the horse isn't dead when it hits the ground; it is concussed, catastrophically.

When its throat is cut its blood makes vapour as it spills from the warm interior of the body, to meet colder ground.

The year before we met I spent a week in the psychiatric ward, on suicide watch. In the interview room, when I lifted my jumper, the admitting doctor winced at the crosshatch along my torso.

You remove your shirt as we work—stupidly bare-handed!—to top the fence with barbed wire, and I watch you, surprised by your visible strength, and for a moment consider you in desire, but the moment passes and I never return to it.

Through the windows of the ward's lounge I saw a billboard edging a nearby four-lane road; it read ESCAPE

You ~~will~~ die a decade later in the same hospital.

The development of the abattoir as a site beyond the boundaries of the city was motivated by a desire on the part of public health inspectors, among others, to remove unregulated private butcheries and slaughterhouses from heavily populated urban areas. It was believed that the visibility of animal slaughter had a morally corrupting effect upon the citizenry, young men in particular.

It felt like we were going crazy then: everyone around me, everyone young. I was eighteen. It was the first year of the new century.

It occurs to me you learnt the same year that you had cystic fibrosis, which should have been diagnosed when you were a baby. At nineteen you were adjusting to a truncated sense of your lifespan.

My housemate had a psychotic break. Friends phoned late, on the landline, self-harming and hazily suicidal. A hospital psychologist advised me to distinguish my own moods from the state of the world.

But what if the problem, I said, *is capitalism?*

The fact that we are shaken together.

I check the word torso in the dictionary and it says: *An unfinished or mutilated thing.*

In the spring, after the hospital, I went to Melbourne to protest a meeting of the World Economic Forum / on Wurundjeri country. 20,000 people showed up, though the cops said half that number.

If our natural curiosity hadn't been carefully repressed, we should quite naturally be very interested in what happens in slaughterhouses, and go and have a look, and not need films like *Le Sang des Bêtes*

A temporary fence had been raised around the whole perimeter of Crown Casino, where the World Economic Forum was scheduled to hold its meeting over three days.

On the first day, a comrade from Chile showed us a tactic they'd used during the years of the junta. Form a circle: it takes less people that way to block a space than it would to block the same with a straight line.

The carousel, or merry-go-round, has its origin in training games practised by Arabic horsemen during the time of the Crusades, from which the idea of circular jousting enters Europe.

It was the era of summit protests, as they were called. In 1999, major demonstrations had taken place in Seattle, outside a meeting of the World Trade Organisation. In 2001, 200,000 people would confront the G8, in Genoa.

Above my desk I keep a postcard reproduction of a photograph by Robert Mapplethorpe, *Two Men Dancing*: a gelatin silver print from a medium-format negative. The two men—still so young, almost boys—are shirtless, perhaps naked (the image is cropped at their waists), and each wears a plastic crown.

Franju and his twin brother Jacques did military service for the occupying French in Algeria.

The summit protests were given binary nicknames after the month and date on which they began. Seattle was N30. Melbourne was S11.

It was twenty-seven years to the day since the coup against Salvador Allende.

In front of the fence, when we have finished building it, we place two signs that we have stolen: REFUGE ISLAND and COMMONWEALTH PROPERTY, DO NOT TRESPASS.

La barricade ferme la rue mais ouvre la voie

We name ourselves The Welcoming Committee.

On 23 May 1871, during the Bloody Week that marked the suppression of the Paris Commune, the Tuileries Palace at the Place du Carrousel was burnt down by the Communards.

Our Chilean comrade said, as we circled in the rain: *We must be a blancmange, encircling the state.*

The second day, the cops waited until past dark to break the picket lines. The media and their cameras had departed. We were rows deep facing off and watching them pull on their leather gloves and I was frightened, but we held, arm to arm along the picket. I could smell the leather jacket of the comrade standing next to me.

As the police chief says to Buñuel's Archibaldo de la Cruz: *If we arrested everyone who'd ever committed a crime in his imagination, there'd be more people in prison than out.*

immobilised, anaesthetised, suspended and bled;

On the third day we danced to be rid of the night before— the pickets cleared by horses, blinkered and foaming, and cops climbing the fence from the inside and walloping people on the head.

Before we met, the year before, I dreamt of police horses: how a group of us were trapped inside a narrow house as the cops rode through, and how they beat us with long-handled instruments.

My first cup of tea in the mourning, you wrote to me once, of the things you liked best.

People were laid out in the road.

There was nowhere to go.

For months afterward we flinched at the sound of helicopters.

If his film had been in colour, said Franju, it would have been unbearable.

The Sydney Morning Herald, 19 April 1848, minutes of the Legislative Council

Mr LOWE presented a petition signed by 1000 citizens of Sydney, praying that the council would take measures for the early removal of the various slaughterhouses from the city, and grant to the proprietors thereof such remuneration as might be adjudged reasonable.

The petition was read and received.

I went to art school thinking: *Start a band, change the world.* This was hopelessly outmoded.

I liked the idea of art school far more than the reality, but then, my idea was a bake of 'Common People' and what I'd read about the Bauhaus.

Der Blaue Reiter and associates, from left: Maria Marc, Franz Marc, Bernhard Koehler, Heinrich Campendonk, Thomas von Hartmann, Wassily Kandinsky.

I applied to art school because of pop music, more or less.

Owing most things in my life to pop music, including an indelible hatred of wage labour.

I was teenage in the 90s and it felt like the answer was to die, but what was the question?

Something to do with shopping centres, something to do with microwaves,

The weekend after leaving the psych ward I went back to work; well, I had to pay the rent.

Bosnia, suburbia, band t-shirts, recuperation, Nokia mobile phones, ads in bus stops, export-processing zones. Have I told the joke about a friend who shelved Tony Blair's memoir in the True Crime section?

What was the question?

I dreamt I went to Woomera again. Dreamt when I was seventeen of an arms dealer waving me behind a curtain and the dust and nausea has never left. Saw a colour plate of

Franz Marc's painting in a book: *Tierschicksale*, The Fate of the Animals; I bring things together but the young stay dead / *stay beautiful*, we used to say. Now I want it to mean *dwell for a time / lightly / in time*, my friends.

Above my desk I keep a Polaroid colour photograph of a silver-white-and-grey tabby kitten sat in the sunlight that falls through a screen door onto the boards of a hallway in the house / on Wangal country where I once lived. The house no longer exists.

I remember now a friend made an artwork called *I sat in the Cafe des Banques*, which no longer exists.

Years after the fact I listen to two former members of the Tute Bianche discuss the G8 protests in Genoa, the protests at which Carlo Giuliani was shot dead by a Carabiniere, but the cops later said that the bullet was deflected by a stone

into his body. The raids and the beatings. Enclosures. Additionally it seems that the rebellion contained some idea that it was possible to rid the world of nobles.

Naturally, the dinosaur unions were there and I wasn't surprised to see schoolchildren ————————————————

———————— highly organised ————————————

Force response officers stormed out of Crown's

circles

in a baton charge

If I invoke the ghosts of redressers past it is because I find myself
afflicted by the sadness of thinking that it is too late to remember
the futures they were dreaming of—including our dreaming of
them—and not wanting to surrender to believing this, I picture
myself hand-in-hand inside a loop of

evenings / the carlight / the sense there isn't time enough /
to stumble / the cash machine / the glow in other people's /
houses / the threshold

moving again
us moving
again moving
against

the violence of the state. I gather
I am gathered in the ghosts round.

    Do you

       dream me like I dream you impossibly
       real again. Lettrists, sisters. My echo   my
       spirits past the screen's mesh
       into the movement of the free. You and me
       in time there isn't time
       enough to stumble. We must fail
       everything failing too late to move fast
       each other again. Past the cash machine.

I didn't tell you that I'm aloud to go to some far distant places but not you.

seriously what about our plan to take over the world. don't think I've forgotten about it.

In front of the fence, when we have finished it, we place two signs that we have stolen: REFUGE ISLAND and COMMONWEALTH PROPERTY, DO NOT TRESPASS.

The white horse is dragged inside the abattoir, and hoisted in chains, the better to enable its exsanguination.

I think we are in our first year when we go below the grounds of our campus, to what would have been the holding cells for patients brought by boat along the Parramatta River to the hospital. Callan Park Hospital for the Insane was built according to the Kirkbride Plan, where the layout of the buildings mimics the wingspan of a bat.

It is the nature of cities to be changed, but I realise now that we moved through Sydney at a time when some tattered things still remained in place: horse racetracks, flour mills, warehouses; these places kept a time, if not a purpose. We entered their time. You and I would just be hanging about and out of this will arise some ordinary adventure.

Pteropus poliocephalus, the grey-headed flying fox—

From the dock, the patients were transported underground.

which now
more frequently drop dead from the trees, overheated—

This would have been around the time of *Tampa*.

I press my hand to the sandstone dividing the holding cells.

nested
in the trees around what was once the asylum.

There must have been many days and evenings when we sat in the shed where you lived / on Gadigal country, or under the frangipani tree that I still think of as your tree, metal chairs grown hot by the sun and beach towels bleaching in the branches, pink frangipani flowers, and yet what we might have said has left me.

Time before, and time before, and always / more time and who is being here before / and always; and what was done, and what gets done.

It might be that the first thing we make isn't the fence inside a gallery, but a fence outside the gallery, in a grassy courtyard of our art school.

I remember the photographs from *Tampa*: hundreds of people lying hot in the shadow cast by shipping containers stacked on deck, which were rust-red.

We paint the letter q onto jumpers, string them up behind that fence. I don't remember this, but it's been remembered to me.

We simply cannot allow ———————————————
————————————————————————

                    asylum seekers

irrespective of the circumstances, irrespective of ——————
——————————————————————

——————————————————————————
————————— stocking —————————————

——————————————————————————
————————————— density —————————

                    a sinking   boat

                                              the Taliban

trying to sail to Christmas Island

—————————————————————————————————

the people ————————————————————————

We don't turn ————————————————————

—————————————————————————————————

————————————————————————————— easy —————————

We climb into overlooked places.

People dismiss the time and space between objects, you write, and I can feel your absence inside of your clothes I have been given now to handle.

The general meaning of *abattre* is *to cause to fall*, or *to bring down that which is standing*.

You build a walkway out of salvaged planks and it moves at jeopardising angles through a house that is afterward demolished for a carpark.

The places we went, which are gone: this is a loss on top of you. I mean a loss additional.

Outside my window / on Bidjigal country a refrigerated truck pulls up and unloads its goods for the butcher.

excised offshore place means any of the following:

(a) the Territory of Christmas Island;

The development of the abattoir as a site beyond the boundaries of the city was instigated by Napoleonic decree on 9 February 1810. Five new locations for the slaughtering of livestock were chosen to replace nearly 400 private butcheries in Paris.

excision time, for an *excised offshore place*, means:

(a) for the Territory of Christmas Island—2pm on 8 September 2001,

Then came the attacks on the World Trade Centre.

It was twenty-eight years to the day since the coup against Salvador Allende.

South China Morning Post, 11 November 1999

Senator Ross Lightfoot, of Western Australia, said illegal immigrants should be quarantined on the Christmas and Cocos islands, distant Australian territories in the Indian Ocean, a suggestion that horrified residents and outraged his parliamentary colleagues.

The senator, who is no stranger to controversy, said creating offshore colonies to house illegal immigrants would 'protect the mainland from disease'.

A new [detention] centre at Woomera in South Australia's north will open within two weeks.

Above my desk I keep a postcard made by a friend and it says: *Another world is possible.*

I'll follow a street to its end for the promise implied in the way that the light falls.

I was teenage in the 90s and it meant being too late for Cabaret Voltaire / the Cabaret Voltaire / Nanterre / Franklin River / Freedom Rides: all that was left was shopping centres, and rock stars swallowing their shotguns.

At hardware stores the salesmen address you and ignore me, assuming that I am the girlfriend. Lots of people make this assumption, which amuses us, and also goes to show that [Redstockings voice] *the hegemony of the couple form must be abolished!*

I was teenage in the 90s and I thought it meant that families, at least, were over.

But there were memories. An elderly gentleman, precisely dressed, gestured to the road that led out from Crown Casino and said: *Sitting on the tram tracks, now that's freedom*, and he meant it.

Sous les pavés, la plage!

Catching a stranger's glance, you write to me once, of the things you like best.

Once we drive through the night / to Ngunnawal country to spend two days spray-painting an empty. Its windows are punctured. We navigate by candlelight. It's freezing in your car held together with whatever and we breathe in rain / spray paint / you swim

What are you like? Once in a New York summer—you are still alive, then—I'm watching Chaplin's *The Gold Rush*: I seem to remember his cabin tipping into the lip of a crevasse, near to oblivion: the young boy sitting next to me laughs so hard he rises up out of his seat and his whole self shivers with laughter. What are you like? When I ride my bike from work shifts to art school and see you the day begins again.

I think of you when I see three sulphur-crested cockatoos wheeling a line across the sky. I think of you when the train lifts from a tunnel and the built world manifests again. I think of you ~~waking in~~ walking in the tunnels; I think of us in derelict houses; I think of the squats I could name but

we weren't too late for / with us or against us or
shop for / weapons or / deserts or / evidence

Franz, wrote the poet Else Lasker-Schüler to her friend Franz Marc, *paint me a green sheep. There is nothing so outlandish left in the world, except me.*

We climb into overlooked places.

The towers were brought down, and Brown men were arrested
for saying or not saying and we said
how many times had we said
on the phone (*we?*)
Bring down the government

The white horse is lowered to the ground, to be flayed. A man
wearing a bloodied apron pumps compressed air in between the
horse's flesh and hide. The white fat below the skin is as enclosing as

This crusade, this ─────────────────────────────

dread on a night when

───────────────── *war on terrorism, is* ─────────────

                               you wake from being pressed into the
hollow of

────────────────────────────── *going to take* ───────

        a loss you cannot name

──────────────────────────────────── *a while*

                        when you awake from it.

Australian ladies and gentlemen, We hope you accept regards and warm
feelings of the miserable and oppressed Afghan refugees turning around
Christmas Island in the middle of the sea,

We must have met around this point, or maybe just before:
September,

while having no shelter,

　　　　your sapling in the pavement and the way the water
sings in the darkroom;

Of course, we are Australian. ─────────────────

　　　　　your laughter.

　　　　　　　　　　　　　　　　　　　　clothes
to change after ten days and even toilet and bathroom.

Christmas Island was excised from the Australian migration
zone on 8 September 2001. People rescued from a sinking
fishing boat by the freight ship *Tampa*—who were mostly
Hazaras, fleeing the Taliban—were forcibly transported by the
Royal Australian Navy to Nauru. The imprisonment of asylum
seekers in island detention centres funded by the Australian
government would be known as the Pacific Solution.

The word comes from the Latin, *solvere*, and retains its etymological
root in the meaning of *solution* as a form of loosening, generally
in liquid, for instance:

William Dampier, the first white man to record a visit to
Christmas Island, owned a slave known as Prince Giolo, whose
real name may have been Jeoly. Prince Giolo was from Miangas,
of the Talaud Islands, in the midst of the Celebes Sea.

　　　　　　　　　　　the salt print, one of the earliest photographic
processes, requires paper to be wetted with a solution of sodium
chloride in water. The paper is then dried.

SIEV—the acronym applied by the Australian government to

asylum seeker boats—has always struck me as too close to *sieve* for coincidence, suggesting that the sea leaks people;

Jeoly was sold by Dampier for exhibition in London and in Oxford.

Suspected Illegal Entry Vessel

                                                    moreover,

sieve as a verb suggests removal.

In London and Oxford, what did he dream of?

Operation Enduring Freedom began on 7 October 2001, with British and United States air strikes against Kabul, Jalalabad and Kandahar.

Which colour of sky? What bird calls?

Wrote Franz Marc to Maria Marc on 14 March 1915, from the war: *How is the woodpecker? Did the pair of red-tails come back?*

Did the pheasant come back?

But I dreamt I went to Woomera again. And sometimes I chase the edges of your presence upon waking.

My main thought now is:

Of course, we are Australian. ————————————————

                        the concept of a new world;

———————————————— We don't behave barbarically.

ISLE OF BATS, VERY LARGE; AND NUMEROUS

TURTLE AND MANATEE

always to create,
to work for the future. Kisses, Franz.

The timing of the *Tampa* incident in the lead up to the 2001 federal election provided an opportunity for a hardline political response to unauthorised arrivals.

In subdued light a solution of silver nitrate is then brushed onto one side of the paper.

Some years after your death I am tasked with sorting out your negatives. I hold the lengths of film up to the sunlight / on Gadigal country: each frame a window on a past that will have happened.

Suspected Unauthorised Non–Citizen

The fact is the children were thrown into water.

Which is not to say the photograph authenticates an event that has existed independent of the photograph. A negative indexes the fullest set of possible solutions to the photograph that ends up being made, but being made, the photograph will frame a truth only the photograph contains.

—— other
SUNCs jumping overboard.

No, well now you are questioning the veracity of what has been said. Those photos are produced as evidence —————————

I am told ———————————————————— it is an absolute fact,
——————————————— into the water.

The way the water sings in the darkroom, and making up the photograph from instruments of light and what we choose—or will have chosen—to leave out of the frame.

There isn't one photograph of us, facing the camera.

The first salt prints have ceased to exist, as they were made before a method to fix the image after exposure had been found.

Alya Satta
Canti beach, South Lampung Regency
Lampung, Sumatra, Indonesia

July 2019

Dear Alya,

I call myself into this space with you.

If you were alive as I write this, you'd be twenty.

I won't flatter myself by imagining that we would know each other, had you lived, or that anything could be redeemed by such a make-believe. I redeem nothing: not in words, not any way.

What is this space? Our movement through it is a falling without landing, and the space has always existed. I call myself into this space but I am always in this space, or will have been; I call myself to the attention of being in this space, which is our differentiation, where I become me, and you you, and will have been, as me and you. And we have fallen together in our separateness that makes all possible; fallen through the space that makes a *we* possible, because there can be you and can be me.

That there was you. But there is no place on this earth now that contains you: you in yourself, irreducible and irreplaceable. In the space of our differentiation is no longer a place—a living place—where we can meet, as you and me, though I have said I will not flatter myself by imagining this meeting, or this place. Perhaps just once, if you had lived, the train I will have been on and yours will pass in opposite directions and a flash of bent heads; and the pylons outside, backs of houses, stubborn flowering weeds on the embankment. Or none of this at all, for your self irreducible was never and could never be contingent on my claims.

Outside my window / on Bidjigal country, the winter sun announces itself along the awnings and my neighbours' roofs, palely. I call this place Sydney, in English, which is my only language. Fence, pale, wall, boundary wall, moat, ditch, trench. Enclose, cordon off, hem, pen, corral. I am told I learnt the names of colours when I was young as you. *Silver. Aquamarine.* These words exactly.

But Alya—can we think the colour without naming it? Does silver exist before *silver*? Clouds, rings, foil, dolphins: these exist, but could they be silver in the absence of the word? And the word in which language? *Blaues Pferd*. I always thought that if a person could imagine a blue horse then it meant a kind of freedom, not just whimsy: the freedom to imagine remaking a world that makes my peace by your death. I have been made by what was done, by what gets done, what I have made, and I can't redeem one part of this.

Alya: I call myself into remembering that I have been always falling through this space, though you have passed from falling with me. There was you, and I will have been, and everything is possible and will remain so in the space that creates you and me—creates *we*—including the failure to remake a world where there is no place now that contains you.

There is nothing in the world that exists that I can point to now and say: *We did this.* Only the documentation: the photographs of street walls, and billboards, and buildings vacated of purpose apart from as repositories of obsolete equipment;

For instance, in one iteration of a travelling retrospective of work by Félix Gonzáles-Torres, *Specific Objects Without Specific Form*, the work *Untitled* (print on red paper, endless copies) was installed near Wassily Kandinsky's *Improvisation 10*.

Having been acquired by art collector and department store heir Franz Kluxen in 1913, *Improvisation 10* passed, in 1918, into the collection of Herwarth Walden, who ran Galerie Der Sturm, an important Berlin exhibition space for artists of the two major pre-war Expressionist groups: Die Brücke, formed in Dresden, and Der Blaue Reiter, founded in Munich. In 1919, *Improvisation 10* was sold to collectors Paul and Sophie Küppers; in 1927 their collection was entrusted on permanent loan to the Provincial Museum of Hannover. This collection was confiscated in 1937 and sold to Ferdinand Möller, one of four art dealers approved by the Nazis for the handling and onward sale of Entartete Kunst, so-called degenerate art. In 1951, *Improvisation 10* was sold to Galerie Beyeler in Basel, Switzerland.

Untitled, as with many works by Gonzáles-Torres, incorporates the possibility of its own dissolution. Viewers— the better word might be *collaborators*—may remove a print or prints from the stack, which may in turn be replenished by whomever is responsible for the work's maintenance, bearing in mind that if new prints are not added, the work will cease to be. Either this, or the work will continue to exist for so long as any part of it is still in the world.

In installation shots from Fondation Beyeler, the red paper of *Untitled* rhymes with the curved red shapes of *Improvisation 10*. The printed words on each sheet of paper echo, too, the black lines of Kandinsky's painting, though one would have to get quite close to the stack in order to read them.

and what
we wrote together, and our maps. The few things we build in
galleries, like the fence, are temporary.

We wanted it this way. *art is not precious, neither is politics*, we
wrote, and we meant (I think we meant) that neither thing
should be remote from the texture of our lives or out of reach
of our making.

Franz Marc's oil painting *The Tower of Blue Horses* was included in the exhibition *Entartete Kunst*, which opened on 19 July 1937, in buildings close to the Munich Hofgarten. A photograph exists of the painting *in situ*, but after protests by veterans of Marc's regiment, who objected to the classification of work by a fallen soldier as degenerate, the painting was removed from the show.

Beginning in 1937, a travelling delegation appointed by the Nazis went to museums throughout Germany, officially stripping them of forbidden artworks. *Der Turm der blauen Pferde* is listed on the typewritten inventory of more than 16,000 artworks confiscated from German museums between 1937 and 1938, and is itemised as no.295 in the subsection of works removed from the Nationalgalerie, Berlin, alongside twenty-two of Marc's handmade postcards, three of his works on paper, and his painting *Three Deer*.

The Nazi inventory, which is in two volumes, arranged alphabetically by city, then museum, then artist, was compiled by the Reich Ministry for Public Enlightenment and Propaganda, and was likely put together in 1942, after sales of selected artworks had been finalised. The two volumes are now held by the Victoria and Albert Museum, London, and remain the only known complete Nazi original of the inventory of artworks confiscated as Entartete Kunst.

There is no entry in the relevant column of the inventory to indicate that *The Tower of Blue Horses* was either destroyed ('X'), sold ('V'), or exchanged ('T'). However, the name *Göring* is entered into an additional column, indicating that the painting was transferred to the custody of Hermann Göring, commander-in-chief of the Luftwaffe, for intended sale on the international art market. But no evidence exists that Göring did sell the painting.

This leads us to conclude—and this may seem a contradiction, on the surface—that our work should be made to disappear.

More than half a million horses were requisitioned in France for military duty during the first week of the First World War. 100,000 or more horses were confiscated for military use during the same week in Britain, but not in Ireland, for fear that the forced removal of working animals would provoke an uprising among the Irish peasantry.

Some military horses, particularly white horses, were painted with camouflage during the war. Colours used for horse camouflage included brown, khaki and sky blue. On the East African front, where soldiers of the British Empire fought those of the German Empire, some horses were painted with zebra stripes.

It is estimated that eight to nine million horses died during the course of the First World War, with the main causes of death being battle injury, starvation and disease. Throughout the war, Britain requisitioned horses for military duty from several of its colonial or former colonial territories, including Australia, while the United States, when it joined the war, exported a significant number of horses to the European theatre. Inevitably, some horses breathed their last on their sea voyages to the battle fronts.

No collectables, no commodities.

If, for example, someone conquers a new colony for his country, the whole country rejoices for him, and does not hesitate—even for a day—to take possession of that colony, Marc writes, in the opening essay of *Der Blaue Reiter Almanac*, which Marc edited with Kandinsky, and which was published in 1912. But the triumphs of The Blue Rider, Marc predicts, will be rejected with anger and abuse. *Why new paintings and new ideas? What can we buy with them?*

And so I remember our work by site, as when

A database search of English-language newspapers for the terms *extraordinary* + *rendition* during the year 2001 returns an article published in the *Boston Globe* on 31 December, about the arrests of two Egyptian asylum seekers in Sweden. Ahmed Hussein Agiza was abducted from a street in Karlstad on 18 December 2001, while walking to a Swedish language class. Mohamed Ibrahim el-Zery was arrested the same day at his workplace, a sweet shop in Stockholm.

In 1999, in Egypt, Agiza had been tried and sentenced in absentia, along with 106 other suspects, to twenty-five years imprisonment for membership of a banned Islamic organisation. Agiza and el-Zery had both left Egypt in 1991, and both claimed to have been subject to harassment, detention and torture by Egyptian security forces during the 1980s. Agiza sought asylum in Sweden in 1999, el-Zery in 2000. There is no indication that the two men knew each other. Their names are given in the *Boston Globe* article as Ahmed Hussein Agaiza and Mohammed Ibrahim al-Zari.

According to a subsequent report published in the *Washington Post* on 29 January 2002, el-Zery was on the phone after his arrest in Stockholm to his Swedish lawyer, Kjell Johnson, when Johnson heard an unidentified voice say *Hang up* and the line went dead. The men were put on a plane on the night of their arrests, before lawyers could lodge an emergency appeal against their removal with the European Court of Human Rights, and sent to Egypt. *US officials have suggested that the practice, known as rendition, may become more common as the antiterrorism campaign unfolds abroad,* reads the initial newspaper report. *Sweden received assurances from Egypt that they would receive a fair trial and they would not be subject to the death penalty.*

I hear a hiss
while walking past the railway underpass where we once spent
a night spray-painting stencils of helicopters, making me think
someone is painting there now, along the wall.

You draw the helicopter stencil from a photograph inside the
federal government's counter-terrorist information pack, sent
to households—

The names Ahmed Hussein Mustafa Kamil Agiza and Mohamed Sulelman Ibrahim el-Zery appear in one of three appendices to the book *Spaces of Disappearance: The Architecture of Extraordinary Rendition*, by Jordan H. Carver, among a list of forty-one known instances of prisoner rendition that were not included in the United States Senate Intelligence Committee report on CIA torture, some findings of which, totalling 525 pages, were publicly released on 9 December 2014, though the rest of the 6,000-page report remains classified. The date of each man's entry into CIA custody is given, in Carver's appendix, as 18 December 2001. It is not known to which site or sites the men were taken after their rendition to Egypt, though based on available evidence, including the testimony of other prisoners who described the acoustic qualities of their cells, it is likely to have been Tora Prison, in Cairo.

The Rendition Project, a research website run by a small group of British academics and human rights lawyers, retains a number of documents relating to the renditions of Agiza and el-Zery, including the known flight path of the CIA-owned Gulfstream Jet V, registration N379P, which took off from Dulles International Airport, Washington D.C., on 18 December 2001, stopped in Cairo to pick up two Egyptian security agents, landed at Stockholm-Bromma Airport at 8.43 p.m. local time, and, one hour and five minutes later, departed again, with Agiza and el-Zery on board, before landing once more in Cairo early in the morning of 19 December.

this is before the invasion of Iraq, but after the
bombing of Afghanistan—

Mohamed el-Zery was released without charge from Egyptian custody on 27 October 2003. In April 2004, Ahmed Hussein Agiza was sentenced by an Egyptian military court to twenty-five years imprisonment for membership of a banned organisation, a sentence that was subsequently reduced to fifteen years. On 8 February 2011, after the fall of the Mubarak government, Agiza was released under a prisoner amnesty deal. A few months later he was granted a Swedish residency permit; his wife and five children had continued to live in Sweden during his imprisonment in Egypt.

Credible evidence exists that both el-Zery and Agiza were subject to torture as a consequence of their renditions by the CIA. Each man was eventually awarded 323,000 euros in compensation by the Swedish government. *Now I will forget everything and look to the future in Sweden for my family and for me*, Agiza told Swedish Radio, upon his return to that country.

and then we strap the spray cans
inside a modified guitar case, to stop them from rattling; I carry it.
I recollect your presence

Further on into the *Almanac*, however, in an essay called 'Die "Wilden" Deutschlands' ('The "savages" of Germany'), Marc is more optimistic when considering the power of those immaterial things, which he calls gifts, offered to the public by his fellow artists. *New ideas kill better than steel and destroy what was thought to be indestructible.* This essay is illustrated by, among other things, a black-and-white photographic plate of a carved wooden statue, captioned *South Borneo*. Notes in an English translation of the *Almanac* further describe it as *Figure of ancestor carved and polished from red-brown rosewood*, and the property of the Ethnographische Abteilung, Bernisches Historisches Museum.

Bern History Museum, in Switzerland, was established in 1894. Part of its Ethnographic Collection consists of items brought back to Europe by John Webber, the official artist aboard HMS *Resolution* during James Cook's third and final voyage across the Pacific. The declared purpose of Cook's voyage, which departed Plymouth on 12 July 1776, was to return Mai, a man from Ra'iātea, in East Polynesia, to his homeland. But the covert purpose of the journey was for Cook to find a navigable route through the Northwest Passage.

Wir reichen ihnen, unbekannt, im Dunkeln unsere Hand, Marc writes, in the conclusion to 'Die "Wilden" Deutschlands', expressing the hope of the artists of The Blue Rider that others will soon join them in the struggle to awaken new ideas for a new age.

We give them our hands, unknown, in the dark.

so suddenly, vividly: your gentleness;
the way you were always proud of me.

We photograph using now obsolete materials:

No records were kept of casualties sustained during the First World War by troops conscripted from the German Empire's colonised populations in East Africa. The soldiers of these territories came from lands now named and bordered as Rwanda, Burundi, and mainland Tanzania.

Kodak / Fuji /
Ilford / Kodak Super8

You scratch the negatives, sometimes, for what the damage
signifies: that the document is not neutral but emerges

Some artworks taken by the Nazis that were not destroyed or sold were stored, during 1941, in the basement of the Ministry for Public Enlightenment and Propaganda, in Berlin, while a significant amount of property and artwork personally looted by Göring was held at Carinhall, his country residence, located in the Schorfheide forest in north-east Germany, near the border with Poland. No sighting of *Der Turm der blauen Pferde* since its transfer to Göring's custody has ever been confirmed. The painting is listed on the Freie Universität Berlin's searchable Entartete Kunst database as *Loss through: Beschlagnahme* (seizure, detention). *Location: unbekannt.* Marc's painting *Three Deer*, which also has Göring's name entered next to it on the inventory, is similarly missing.

Today, Schorfheide forest is a biosphere reserve.

The question remains—there is no inventory to account for it—as to how many of the more than two million objects in the permanent collection of the Victoria and Albert Museum were also stolen from their owners.

from our
hands, our fumbling and clumsy hands, you write.

HIMMLER   *HATE*

HOLE   *HELMS*

are the words printed onto each sheet of red paper that makes Gonzáles-Torres' work *Untitled*.

After depletion the stack may be rendered again.

When searching the Congressional record of Senator Jesse Helms, Republican member for North Carolina from 1973 to 2003, I find, along with his introduction of the AIDS Control Act of 1987, which aimed to prohibit HIV-positive aliens from immigration or travel to the United States, an entry for his co-sponsorship of Special Joint Resolution 131, introduced to the Senate on 14 July 1983, designating the week of 18–24 September that year as Cystic Fibrosis Week.

There isn't one photograph of us, facing the camera.

Retrospectively, it has become more obvious to me—though we were not unaware of it, then—that the artists we admired were, by and large, people who'd died young. Such an impulse isn't rare at age nineteen, but for you at least, an early death was neither an abstraction nor a romance.

The exocrine glands affected by cystic fibrosis include the bronchi, the intestines and the pancreas. *Exocrine* comes from the Greek: *krinein*, to separate.

And yet I cannot say you wholly died of this.

You loved the artist Gordon Matta-Clark, who cut into buildings—who split a house in half.

I change tense, and travel back across your death's border.

You love the artist Gordon Matta-Clark.

Wrote Franz Marc to his friend Paul Klee on 12 June 1914: *I'm still convinced that I won't paint my best pictures until I'm forty or fifty; I'm not yet ready in myself for this.*

I don't think I ever grasped the full implications of your illness, which was chronic and progressive, while you lived. It was easy not to think about.

Having sought autonomy, which I have thought meant holding to the chance that I might kill myself, my life has been remote;

Matta-Clark's Super8 film *Splitting, 1974,* begins

as if it took place in rooms apart from me

with a tilt-shot up the front steps to a notice at the entrance to a house that reads: DO NOT OCCUPY.

and only years later do I realise I was there.

I knew that you would die young. I didn't know it at all.

I'm not yet ready in myself for this.

Marc wrote this to Klee six weeks before the outbreak of the First World War, into which he and his friend August Macke would be drafted immediately.

Sunlight burns through the aperture of Matta-Clark's split house; the fissured masonry cants the floor to a new slope.

I think it's before the invasion of Iraq but after the bombing of Afghanistan when we cut the word *terrorist* out of the newspaper and blow it up, on the photocopier, so that each

t e r   o   i s

is big enough to trace separately, while preserving the erosion of the dot matrix caused by our enlargement, each letter at its edges now an archipelago, which we then cut into stencils, using scalpels, in the shed where you live / on Gadigal country, its tin roof ticking in the rain, until all the ink is negative space.

Though the word *outbreak* suggests the war was a sickness beyond human agency to either prevent or amend, which it was not.

Then we take the stencils into an enclosed courtyard behind the colour darkrooms, which were once the isolation cells, and make the word again, over and over, spray-painting the letters in their signifying order onto lengths of paper, and, when these are done, rolling them up, and in the morning cover over a billboard that edges a four-lane highway next to the freight terminal and the airport, close to the house in which I live,

Félix Gonzáles-Torres died of AIDS-related illnesses on 9 January 1996, aged 38. He had been born in Cuba, where, in 1991, the United States government established a detention camp for HIV-positive Haitian refugees at the US naval base, Guantanamo Bay.

you and I and two comrades, the four of us, with rollers and a ladder and a bucket of wallpaper glue. We wear white overalls.

Years later in New York / on the lands of the Lenape I listen to two former members of the Tute Bianche discuss the G8 protests in Genoa. They recall that in the months leading to the protests, they had talked among themselves about the peasant revolts of medieval Europe, by way of inspiration. Only, those revolts were defeated. *And so we were slaughtered,* they said;

By repeating the word terrorist *over and over, we were trying to expose the word for what it is*, you write, *a dangerous weapon.*

Marc supported the war, at least at first, in the belief that it would be the cataclysm necessary to usher in modernity.

take *care whose ghosts you invoke.*

Tear up the road with shot; throw corpses and horses into all the fountains, wrote Touissant Louverture, nearly a decade into the Haitian revolution begun by slaves and former slaves, after declaring himself ruler for life and after Napoleon's invasion of 1802: *burn everything and annihilate everything in order that those who come to reduce us to slavery may before their eyes see the image of that hell which they deserve.*

The towers were brought down. Friends phoned late, on the landline, and we watched, and watched and watched.

A part of my initial reaction was a feeling that chickens had come home to roost; but how easy it is to use an animal idiom in order to diminish the complexity of human loss,

I dream of cavalcades of emptied rooms.

                                                           as if animals
are any less complex, or deserve their lives less.

The more time has passed the more unbearable I find that day's footage, being not nineteen or cavalier anymore with the idea of my life or anyone's, and knowing now what has come after.

The last Siberian crane reported seen in Afghanistan was shot dead in 2002.

Of all the eerie things about that infernal loop |: plane hitting tower | plane hitting tower :| the eeriest is the noiselessness of the impact as recorded by a fixed camera at a distance.

We think our billboard will be loud but it is quiet.

We think

We will make no distinction

        we think

        between the terrorists

   no   ist

   not enough

        we think

        no distinction

   between

        you're

   not enough

        planted

   between

Concrete decision in favour of the victory of light in real possibility is the same as countermove against failure in process.

I keep these words above my desk, between the postcard reproduction of Mapplethorpe's *Two Men Dancing* and a torn photocopy of a nineteenth-century portrait—a daguerreotype, I think—of two young girls, touching hands, who face the camera with a hard intensity. We were rows deep, watching the cops pull on their gloves, and I was frightened, but we held, arm-to-arm along the picket.

there are no blockades without trust, you write, about the all-of-us.

We write: *there is no collaboration without friendship.*

Sometimes just for seconds the extent of my grief for you reveals itself and my breath dissolves, because it has no edges at all, and I turn over in the water, which is where this sensation most occurs, when it occurs, and think of my aliveness as it travels in the water, and sunlight that moves through the water, which leaves eventually, though I cannot see where or draw a line if I were asked to.

Did you ever have the dream that I did, after you died, of being inside the ocean, and, looking up, a pod of whales—all the weight of them revoked by water. And what did that look like from your side? For weeks after your death my hands shook continuously.

It's flattering to think that we were fated to meet but I tend to think that fate is what we make out of chance; we can be actors within history. I'm writing this for you upon the hope that—as with an album by a band championed by John Peel in 1986, or similar, the liner notes hand-typed and a PO box to write to— the hope still sung by these things is *we have existed*.

We exist.

We exists.

Is this naive? I think we shared some fundamental naivety—not the same as innocence—that making things could be enough, one heart joined to the next

and I think I still believe it. As I sit in my kitchen / on Bidjigal country and listen to the house breathe, planes trace their routes overhead, and in these unearned hours think

what it might be

to live

> without the wage / without the state / without
> the penitentiaries / to be
>
> unafraid / to be / freely
> indebted to each other.

Dear brother, my sister:

When the call came that you had cancer, I was sitting / on Gadigal country looking east across the ocean.

My ancestors must have been seen from this coastline: convicts unloading from the ships. History's contingency does not diminish, in its contingency, the violence that would bring me to this place: a succession of enclosures that's cast us onto the market but not equally imperilled, and far from togetherness.

I never saw you alive again.

Like watching television three years before we met and the dogs on the waterfront, the stevedores locked out; picket lines but everyone who didn't work on the docks forbidden from striking, lest that turn into something.

Nor did I see you dead, and I have wondered since, would it have helped to have the fact of this |: body in my mind | to not be saying this :| goodbye.

no document can make you manifest;

ISLE OF BATS, VERY LARGE; AND NUMEROUS TURTLE AND MANATEE

Above my desk I keep a black-and-white photograph I took of you from when we first climbed into the tram sheds, behind the harness-racing track in Glebe, across the harbour from what had been the asylum.

I remember the place as enormous, with holes in the roof—whole colonies of pigeons must have lived there where the weather leaked in and the sound of whomever was graffitiing rose through the rafters to the sky.

Voyez, ces oiseaux blancs, sing the workers of La Villette abattoir in Franju's film, and the blood puddled along the floor is silver as the crystals in a film's emulsion.

La mer qu'on voit danser
Le long des golfes clairs
A des reflets d'argent,

After you died, someone said to me that objects are just objects, referring to things that had been made by you for me, like the book of images, mostly cut from contact sheets, that you glued onto card and interspersed with your drawings then sewed into a mesh binding, the whole thing smaller than a matchbox, and I knew that our friendship, being friendship, had been judged as insubstantial.

Dear brother, my sister:

After clearing the Selat Sunda—the strait that lies between Java and Sumatra, through which the ships of the Dutch East India Company once sailed, in a roughly north-east direction, to plunder the Moluccas, for their spices—there is nothing, heading south, but Christmas Island,

> no document
>
>   and nothing south of

it but Antarctica. Only the ocean.

La mer,
Des reflets changeants
Sous la pluie.

Operation Relex was the military and naval blockade used to enforce the transportation—or, preferably, the *turnback*— of asylum seekers in the wake of *Tampa*. For its duration, photography of said asylum seekers was discouraged.

——————— people back into the sea,

In summer once, I saw a polar bear, in the Bronx Zoo; it had a little swimming pool: the walls of it the colour of the idea of *ocean* in a child's drawing.

When it suited though, photographs from Operation Relex were leaked to the media, like the ones allegedly depicting children thrown into the water by their parents, which in fact showed no such thing.

Those photos are produced as evidence ———————————
——————————————

And I thought that I might find you, in the ocean, that my grief's solution was the sound of you as it persisted in the water even after you were buried in the earth.

Almost all film stocks contain a gelatin emulsion. Gelatin is manufactured from the hides and hooves of animals.

Now I want to start as a child would, Marc wrote to his friend August Macke, *in the landscape with three colours and a few lines, rendering my impression of it using only these...so that the working process consists of adding rather than subtracting.*

I think of my skin: the only border between who might be this self I can conceive of and the world; my animal within the world.

I thought the polar bear must have been the loneliest creature.

When I knew you would die it was too late to find a chance to press your skin against mine, and I feel it—your absence radiating as the belly of a beast might leave a shallow in the ground that traps the notion of its being there but not the thing in being there itself, in all its living heat.

This bitter earth, sings Dinah Washington, at the end of Charles Burnett's feature film *Killer of Sheep,* as a real sheep is winched by pneumatic hoist into position for its real death: *well, what a fruit it bears.* Inside the abattoir, Stan, played by Henry Gale Sanders, whups sheep into line for their journey to the kill floor. I think the scene both is and isn't a metaphor for the annihilation of the Middle Passage.

Sanders had fought in Vietnam.

Just as Franju's film, released in 1949, cannot help but also be a commentary on the Occupation, and on who—as with the sheep that leads its fellows to the slaughter, sensing that its own life is spared—will betray whom.

I have yet to lie down on the pavement and refuse to rise in sorrowing for any of this.

What good is love, sings Washington, who died aged 39, *that no one shares?*

There is no collaboration without friendship.

The second time we climb into the tram sheds—when we hold a tea party inside a tram that still boasts a framed portrait of the queen—we take the chance to rifle through one of the open shipping containers where the harness-racing track has jettisoned its stuff.

From shore to shore!

I dreamt I went to Woomera again.

We simply cannot allow a situation to develop where Australia is seen around the world as a country of easy destination.

On or around 18 October 2001, a wooden fishing boat set sail through the Sunda Strait, heading south from Canti beach, Sumatra, sinking the next day or thereabouts somewhere in waters past the care of any nation. Forty-five people survived, out of an estimated 400 people onboard who were seeking asylum. Kawthar Satta was five years old; her sister, Alya, two. They drowned.

Inside my dream, the place is grassy as a country town: a church, a mess hall, a sense of sandstone and a river out of sight. The air is steeped in purpose, we are here to clean this place—no, to cleanse it. (*we?*)

Gelatin is a colloid: a particulate material that can be suspended in water or other solute without settling. It disperses the light-sensitive silver halide crystals in a film's emulsion, and prevents them from adhering to each other.

The boat that sank on or around 19 October 2001 was assigned the name SIEV X.

Sweep floors, pull weeds, pack artefacts in boxes:

I remember the headlines, yet more marches.

everyone moves with resoluteness. But I cannot find a purpose. Something like contrition rasps away at me.

On 12 September 1914—two weeks before August Macke would be killed by artillery fire—Franz Marc wrote to Maria:

OF THE FEASIBLENESS AND PROBABLE ADVANTAGE OF SUCH A SETTLEMENT FROM THE NEIGHBOURING GOLD AND SPICE ISLANDS

The question of why the boat known as SIEV X was not detected by Australian navy ships or reconnaissance planes deployed in Operation Relex, before it sank—even though the boat had been noted by Australian military intelligence, and photographed, before it left Sumatra—has never been answered.

———————————— We don't behave barbarically.

Battles,
wounds, motions, all appear so mystical, unreal, as though they meant
something quite different from what their names say—yet everything
is still coded in a terrifying muteness—or my ears are deafened by the
noise, so that I cannot yet distinguish the true language of these things.

Inside my dream, a friend has left a zine pinned to a wall, and when I pull it down to read, an image on the page bursts into flames, you remember, all the Super8 we shot and then ran through projectors in perilous loops, until it burnt.

From inside the shipping container we steal photographs of horses, which are damaged: ghost horses, water horses, the track they're moving on dissolved by dampness over time.

And I imagine the animals, dispersed through the photographs I've made, their skins the emulsion that my image is sieved through.

Of course, we are Australian. ⸻⸻⸻⸻⸻

We don't turn people back into the sea,

You took a photograph once / on Gadigal country of all the news photographers photographing some peripheral scuffle; perhaps it was on George Street and I think it was one of those May Days when, for a brief few years, there was a protest on May 1 instead of just the nearest Sunday when the unions lead a march through the city. On at least one of these we staged a blockade of the offices of G4S, the multinational security company that owned the Wackenhut Corporation, a subsidiary of which, Australasian Correctional Management, ran the mainland immigration detention centres.

That day, the cops brought horses in to break the picket line— into a confined space that might have been the entrance to a car park, from memory—and several people were injured, but hours before that, in the morning, a passing office worker had bought us all coffee and doughnuts. I believe in all of us. I don't see how anything can change, if we don't. At the hospital I was given crutches for the sake of my foot, which had been crushed by a horse.

At night, the corridors of our art school's photographic department felt especially austere, echoes clapping off the battleship-grey walls, the windows small and placed too far above head-height and barred. This wing, the one furthest away from the front gates, was what had been the men's high security ward when the place was an asylum. The darkrooms—the ones for colour chemistry—were the isolation cells. Each time that I ~~would~~ open the door after minutes spent feeling in the dark to see you again in the corridor after you have opened your door is a surfacing. A site retains the depths of its history.

Beneath Pitt Street, parallel to George Street, where I first had a job in a shop that no longer exists, there runs a freshwater tributary—colonists called it the Tank Stream—progressively enclosed, then paved over.

I was seventeen, then. The day would pass and I'd only see the sky if I hurried to Hyde Park on my lunch break. Sometimes I think I meet myself there, forgetting—or not quite grasping—the fact that when Guy Debord graffitied *Ne travaillez jamais* on a wall along the rue de Seine he had an inheritance to live on. Wasn't wrong, though. Wage labour is the robbery of time.

Above the stream but below street level, down the stairs to the inside of a bookshop that no longer exists, I would stand at the counter, looking over at the scars on the wrists of another teenage girl who also worked as a cashier (say *stars*, say I find you in the exosphere), but couldn't figure out what to say to her, nor to a stockroom worker or even express to myself that I was bothered by his hands pressing lightly against me. Pitt Street is named after William Pitt the Younger, Prime Minister of Britain when the penal colony of Sydney Cove was established by invasion, in January 1788. One year later came the French Revolution; two years after that, the revolution in Haiti. Pitt's government, fearing Jacobin activity, passed the Seditious Assemblies Act on 18 December 1795, banning gatherings of more than fifty people, while the Combination Acts of 1799 and 1800 forbade *all contracts, covenants and agreements whatsoever...at any time...heretofore made...between any journeymen manufacturers or other persons...for obtaining an advance of wages...or for lessening or altering their or any of their usual hours or time of working, or for decreasing the quantity of work.*

I tried to do as little as possible.

In years since I've seen him sometimes, my harasser, my workmate, drawing in chalk on the pavements. I have not given him the change I could afford to give.

All revolutions run into history, yet history is not full; unto the place from whence the rivers of revolution come, thither they return again.

Say the word *dog*.
That word is just a noise that you make with your tongue and
your throat.
Say *missing*. Say *lost*.
Or the way the water sings
in the darkroom, if we are

(*we?*)

if we are

to be

everything:

I listen to an interview with Amrit Wilson, recalling the two-
year strike, begun in 1976, by workers at the Grunwick Film
Processing Lab, in London: *At the height of the pickets there were
20,000 people there—against employers, in a way against the state.*

But it was something which, somehow, it was let go of.

We have to face it, the left didn't have any strategies.

Much of history is about important and famous people—kings and presidents and generals of armies. When you think of what happened to you yesterday, as well as to all the other people in the whole world, that is history. It is something in time past

the stormwater drainage pit built nearly a century ago / on Wangal country to stop Sydenham from flooding. It used to be a swamp round here. A few ducks will scud along the residue of water and I'm always looking out in case today's the day someone decides to take a raft, or even a rowboat, into the pit. There's a shot in *Le Sang des Bêtes* where a freight barge appears to sail through a field, because the camera has been placed low enough to obscure the canal, and when I see a shipping container beached behind a chainlink fence on the street that runs beside the drainage pit to the shopping centre, I think of it: that shot, what's hidden. Ravens like it here, veering from fences, and towels hang at the brothel's rear entrance; the walls are candy pink. In Basel where I went to see Franz Marc's painting *Tierschicksale* I found myself walking down a street where people were purchasing sex but didn't realise it at first. A man tried to buy my services and was pissed off when I ignored him; I recognised his tone even if I didn't understand the words. I wasn't afraid: it just made me think about the fact that I was ignorant of the city and its languages. Most businesses around here aren't open to the public though, being wholesalers or factories for one specific product or another, dumplings or cash registers, the foil-stamping place. Think of all the toothpaste boxes: someone in one of these factories once designed the die that was then used to stamp the packaging so, inside the supermarket inside the shopping centre, shimmering boxes will persuade us that our teeth are gonna shine. Some of these buildings, or parts of them, also used to be punk venues, and young men—it was rarely women—would set up their gear on the floor and perform to maybe twenty people, then roll out of town. It's easy to romanticise, especially when none of this will make the history books. Across the road from the rear entrance to the shopping centre is the fence from which we stole the sign that read COMMONWEALTH PROPERTY, DO NOT TRESPASS. I think of you walking past this fence; I mean I think of you whenever I walk past it, until the fence is gone, which it is, now, there having been more time elapsed since I began this than might seem. I think about the fact that the summit protests got crushed by policing, and, after September 2001, a deliberate conflation of dissent with terrorism by the ruling class that still exists. The shopping centre is expanding and the driverless train line is going in. Past the drained pit (and where did the ducks go?) along what was a hopscotch of stormwater channels and the loading bays of factories is now a casting site for the driverless train line: crescent stacks of tunnel parts, sand piles. (Beneath the pavement, the beach?) Making the brutishness of *free trade*—so often abstracted as the will of the market—evident: that's where our protests succeeded. Bags of dead piglets will be sent to the incinerator; others lie forgotten in the stalls. But outside of our appointed confrontations with a fraction of the ruling class, we had no strategy—not in the workplace, or at the distribution points of trade (docks, rail, roads, warehouses), where capital is vulnerable—to last beyond the protests getting crushed. Where the shopping centre is was once a tannery.

dear anywn, you write to me,

my dyslexia has got a good memory.

I changed the spelling of my name—and you are dead by then—
and said to everyone that I was sick of mispronunciations, but I
think that what I've wanted is a space between me and me. Your
death took the best of me. Most of our work was anonymous,
and if I claim it now I still want to say we could have been
anyone.

Could we have been anyone?

call Anwyn 4pm, I find written on the back of an envelope,
when I am sorting through your things.

I'd been looking for a drawing of yours on a telephone pillar nearby, because your characters—scratched in a few spare seconds, with their daydreaming expressions—are as intrinsic to my sense of who you might have been as is your handwriting, and the fact that some of them are still scattered through the city means to me that the city has remembered you to me, in what was once wet concrete, and telephone pillars. It isn't that you are childish but that you take imagination seriously, as a child might: as something to be borne with the whole heart. What are you like? In the middle of the night you leave a drawing done on scrap plywood by my doorstep. In the house where I lived with the silver-grey cat and the bellies of planes almost touching the yard we would talk on the phone just so long as one line or another hadn't been disconnected, and yours often had. I remember the grass in the yard being burnt by the summer that preceded the invasion of Iraq, and the banners that got painted on bedsheets; the meetings and running down streets and the ad hoc murals the two of us make of helicopters and police dogs and the faces of the war's chief hawkers. 'Lose Yourself' is on the radio and at my place we're listening to *Yanqui U.X.O.*—the rear sleeve diagrams the corporate connections between major record labels and the arms industry. I can't find your drawing where it used to be, past the shopping centre up the hill to where the second-hand white goods store clings on and the wall by the bus stop will always sport the remnant of some poster or another: AUTOMATION AND THE WORKING CLASS: WILL MACHINES REPLACE US? I've been looking at job advertisements. ALDI is after employees with a *positive attitude and hardworking spirit*, Priceline wants someone who possesses *a true passion for cosmetics*. The narrator of *Le Sang des Bêtes* says that the horse's hooves will become fertiliser, and its bones will be made into bone black, or ladies' toiletries; the film's commentary was written by Jean Painlevé, anarchist and credited 'ant handler' on Buñuel's *Un Chien Andalou*. At the veterinary clinic, in the waiting room, I overhear a man say to his daughter: *They don't feel pain like we do*. A greyhound trembles between them. The initial airstrike on Baghdad by US forces consisted of thirty-six Tomahawk missiles and two F-117-launched 'bunker busting', laser-guided GBU-27 bombs, manufactured by Raytheon, an updated version of which, GBU-28, was later sold to Israel for airstrikes against Hezbollah in Lebanon. Tomahawk missiles have also been deployed by US forces in Afghanistan as part of Operation Enduring Freedom, and, more recently, in bombings of Yemen and Syria. Your drawing must have been painted over. When the bombing of Iraq began some dolt with a megaphone admonished a bunch of us for jumping up and down as we stood outside Town Hall waiting for the protest to begin to move / on Gadigal country. *This march will be disciplined*, they said, and we said—we taunted—*discipline's for armies*. Nothing we made was meant to last. Nothing we made has lasted for as long as what we made by making together. In the house that no longer exists near the airport and the freight terminal, I grew into the habit of sleeping with a cargo of stuff in my bed: shoes, alarm clocks, dictionaries, razor blades; the cat, too, her flawless white paws, her warmth steady and bounded as a stone in the sun. MUTINY, our banners read: TURN THE GUNS AROUND.

I didn't tell you that I'm aloud to go to some far distant places but not you, you write to me, but never send, before I leave for New York. You and your life's love had already gone to Gija country.

Arriving in New York I felt a Technicolor unreality. A yellow cab swept me across what must have been the Queensboro Bridge and it was August; and sunshine delineated everything a little too brightly, but different to the bottom-of-the-world glare I knew. This light had ambition, I was sure, as it picked up the edges of the brick apartment blocks parked by the East River and the river's moat, and Art Deco buildings glinting silver as nickels in the sun, in that sun; even the cab I was in felt haloed by an extra-yellowness. It was jet-lag, and arriving / on the lands of the Lenape as far away from what I knew as I could never guess I'd get; a windfall, material and sudden, maybe also spiritual, if this isn't too gauche a word and even if it is, the scholarship girl's condition is to know her luck and to fail to conceal it.

seriously what about our plan to take over the world

On Gadigal country / I come across a nineteenth-century terrace on the road leading down to the tram sheds—now a *food precinct*—and the internal floors and walls are gone, but on an external wall at the third-storey height is an intact stained-glass window, and, in the opposite wall, in what would have been the room above the cellar, is a tiny grate fireplace bordered with blue-and-white tiles. A young woman lived here once I imagine and thought of the light on the water what's close to these houses. She's drawing her hands to the fire. If you were alive, we'd make something: I picture us stacking all the bits we might need like spray cans or rollers in the back or on the roof of your blue station wagon that was always more scrapyard than car. You and I will just be drifting about and out of this will arise some ordinary adventure, like the song 'Being Boring', by Pet Shop Boys, which is about what happens when you want to find a way past the humdrum but, by virtue of its title, is also about not trying to, and how these things are intertwined. *Tierschicksale* was damaged in 1917 when a Berlin warehouse belonging to Galerie Der Sturm caught fire; Marc was dead by then—killed by shrapnel, at Verdun—so the painting was restored by his friend Paul Klee. She thought of the sun on the water; the bay would've stunk when she lived here. With things that were made and unmade there. Wool scour, slaughterhouse, piggery. You got loose of gravity—I read that the Thwaites Glacier might collapse, the ice will crash into the sea with the thunder of horses—and what is that like when it leaves? 'Being Boring' is about what we had done and then you're gone to not never being boring with me. The edge of the undamaged portion of Marc's canvas is raised above the damaged part, which sinks like an old scar, and occupies about one-third of a painting nearly two metres high and more than two-and-a-half metres in width, and which has a muddy tinge—perhaps caused by smoke, or by water used to put out the fire—that Klee either could not remove or chose not to. Credit Suisse is the financial partner of the Kunstmuseum Basel, where the painting hangs, and one of the world's largest investment banks. It hosts the annual McAleese/Credit Suisse Defense Programs Conference, to showcase weapons research; for instance, the hypersonic missile, intended to be capable of travelling at fifteen times the speed of sound. An ordinary passenger jet can reach Cleveland, Ohio from Washington D.C. in thirty minutes; in the same amount of time, hypothetically, a hypersonic missile launched from Washington D.C. could land in Micronesia. *He was more humane than I am, more openly affectionate, more explicit about everything*, Klee wrote in his journal after Marc's death, and I could say the same about you, which makes me wonder if the living share a tendency to imbue the dead with goodness, perhaps especially when the young grieve the young, for in these cases we have scarcely had time to disappoint each other. Or if what I recognise in Klee's remembrance is the loss of proximity to graciousness. I felt a kind of craziness that nothing could be done to stop the war. At the start of meetings we would ask for the undercover cops to identify themselves and leave, and of course they never did this and of course they were there. The other joke that was only partly a joke was that the phone line in my house was tapped.

been sussing out good hiding places for when we are fugitives, you write to me.

Some weeks after your death when I returned to the flat where I lived opposite the last working container dock in Brooklyn, everything was just exactly as I'd left it. (Chris Lowe is a genius, I think, because he's spent a career in Pet Shop Boys not doing anything. I saw them play once: while Neil sang, Chris turned his head from side to side. That was it.) Really I thought that in the interim the furniture should have wrecked itself, or some creature risen out of the Hudson to expire upon my floor. I hung a black-and-white photograph I'd taken of you once in your kitchen / on Gadigal country by my door but barely stepped outside for months. The title of Marc's 1913 painting, *Tierschicksale*, was Klee's coinage, and has also been translated as *Animal Destinies*. Marc changed his mind about the war. *We must unlearn, rethink absolutely everything in order to come to terms with the monstrous psychology of this deed and not only to hate, revile, deride, and bewail it, but to understand its origins and to form counter-thoughts.* There are still patches of France along what was the Western Front—where the Battle of Verdun was fought for twenty-four hours short of ten months—where nearly nothing lives: the unexploded ordnance and chlorate from the mustard gas contaminates the earth. I keep returning to the view of the Hudson as it opens to the ocean and me sat hours in tracing. The paths through the window. Of barges, freight ships, liners, and the ferry yellow as a taxi. Feral cats fleet between container stacks: I watch them, the gantry cranes, their pterodactyl bearing; the weight of you somewhere behind me now; time we fell through left hanging.

Neil: [Our manager] Tom was always—and probably still is, for all I know—obsessed with thinking that Chris and I were lovers, and quite simply couldn't believe that we weren't. He said to me, '*Everybody* knows…'

Chris (amused): That's classic Tom.

Neil: And I'd say, 'Everyone may know, Tom, but in actual fact it's not true.' And he'd say, 'Everyone will know why he's in the group—this is going to do you no good at all' and he suggested it would be better if I went it alone. I said that I couldn't go it alone, there are *two* of us.

two years—thats too long, you wrote to me but never sent before
I left and you are right, you run out of life.

Instead, you send me a postcard:

I hope this gets to you before you leave.

> *I still have this letter*
> *I don't know why I haven't sent it.*
> *I suppose I want it to be*
>> *really special and I m having*
>> *trouble. anyway   I love you and think of you often.*

The bells of the Münster filled the air on the morning when I went to see Marc's painting in Basel; it was Pentecost: the feast that celebrates the Apostles' sudden fluency in tongues, thanks to the grace of the Holy Spirit. In the Kunstmuseum, I hold myself as close as I can to the canvas; at this distance, the painting is all paint, as all words are phonemes and all music is waves. Marc thought that art would one day convey the world *as the forest and the horse feel themselves to be, in their essence.* Despite his posthumous banning as degenerate, the yearning in his paintings for a perfect state of nature—apart from a few works into which history has entered—could be interpreted, and has been, as foreshadowing the Reich that aimed to reign over Germany, eternally, destroying all history, all change. Then I think of Ernst Bloch on the Expressionists: *Anyone who had ears to hear could hardly have missed the revolutionary element their cries contained.* Mostly I prefer Marc's watercolours to his paintings, especially the postcards made for Else Lasker-Schüler, which portray the animals that lived in her imaginary land of Thebes. These have a fluidity of line that I sense corresponds to the speed of the animal's conception on the paper, and because of this alacrity of gesture, time is palpable in them in a way it almost never is in his oil paintings. The latter seek the stasis of paradise, and I think the slowness of working in oil paint partly accounts for this. On the verso of a postcard made for Else Lasker-Schüler, on which he sketched his tower of blue horses for the first time, Marc wrote: *Write or telephone us, will you?* And elsewhere, *sister,* and elsewhere: *my dear friend.*

In the centre of Marc's painting *Tierschicksale* is a blue deer: she's calling from the centre of the painting. And when I first saw it in a book, when I was younger than I would be when we met, I felt the century condense. And all my dread condensed.

The tree that falls towards her is in facets of red-violet; a gold fire burns within its trunk. I read that a live export ship has sunk, that birds are falling from the sky, flycatchers and warblers. Three billion animals have burnt in this place bordered as Australia since I began this, and the fact that all the sound of it is dampened by the painting being paint—well, it haunts me.

Cancer is what? Asbestos / solvents / radiation / sun / smoke / formaldehyde / fucking luck, like us meeting. With cystic fibrosis, what chance did you have?

So I'd come back to summer in Sydney and you came back from Warmun: we hadn't seen each other for three years. You were ill and I'd been starving myself into danger, the threat of the psych ward again, but I hadn't told you this and so betrayed a trust I should've trusted in.

I am telling you now.

I didn't tell you
that your leg-up
over the fences,
your bullet belt
for pencils, your football socks,
your cough,
that your almost inevitable
young death, listen,
my heart is

Years after the fact I learn that the silos we climbed on Glebe Island—behind the Anzac Bridge, halfway across the harbour between what was the art school and the harness-racing track—sit on the site of the city's first abattoir. Somewhere, a black-and-white photograph: the side of my face in the wind as it blew across the roof of the silos, which you must have taken.

Cattle were driven on foot to the abattoir from as far away as Coonabarabran, 450 kilometres north-west of the city. The direction of their travel, back over the mountains dividing the plains from the coast, was opposite to that of the colonists only decades prior. The site of the Glebe Island abattoir was finalised in 1852. The first of the white surveyors ventured onto countries past the mountains—Wiradjuri country, Gamilaraay country—in 1818.

COMMONWEALTH PROPERTY, DO NOT TRESPASS.

cattle / *noun*. MIDDLE ENGLISH

[from Anglo-Norman, Old Northern French *catel* var. of Old French *chatel* CHATTEL.]

I   Property.
1.   (Personal) property; wealth, goods. ME–L15.
2.   A chattel. L15–E18.

A tally of livestock in the colony of Sydney Cove, dated 1 May 1788, ninety-six days after invasion, lists one stallion, three mares, three colts, two bulls, five cows, twenty-nine sheep, twenty-five pigs, five rabbits, thirty-five ducks and eighty-seven chickens. Many of these animals had been taken aboard when the fleet docked for provisions at the Cape of Good Hope. Others breathed their last on the voyage.

The tally—*Enclosure No. 1* in Governor Arthur Phillip's letter to Baron Sydney, Leader of the House of Commons—notes that three sheep are dead, and the cows and bulls have been lost.

II   Treated as *pl.* Livestock.
3.   Animals of the genus *Bos*, oxen; (now *arch. & dial.*) livestock, (in stables) horses. ME.

When you say *cow,* you're using a word from Old English. Saxon farmers called it a *cu*. The Norman lords who ate the *cu* for dinner called the meat *boef.*

4.   *contempt.* People (likened to cattle). *arch.* L16.

By the 1830s, the governing class of the New South Wales colony had lost control both of livestock and of squatters— some of them convicts who had served out their sentences, but most of them wealthy free settlers—occupying land beyond the borders of the colony. *An Act further to Restrain the unauthorised occupation of Crown Lands, and to provide the means of defraying the expense of a 'Border Police'* was drafted in February 1839, and approved that April by the Legislative Council.

The Act allowed for settlers who occupied land without a government license (*analogous to rent*, wrote Governor George Gipps) to be fined, and for tax to be raised per head of cattle, sheep and horse to pay for the Border Police.

Aux Porte de Paris, reads the opening caption of *Le Sang des Bêtes*. At the gates of Paris.

As we climbed the ladder to the roof of the silos, the city would thin into brightness.

Why did we climb them?

Because we were young and not afraid of falling.

And when I knew you would die, I looked across the water to the silos and thought of us, there on the roof of the city—stood up there as if we were the secret in it all.

You mentioned the waste in weight;—what waste would there be upon a beast travelling 300 miles to market, including the road over the Blue Mountains—what would a 900 lb. beast weigh when it reached the Abattoir, after travelling 300 miles?

Outside my window / on Bidjigal country, a refrigerated truck unloads its goods for the butcher. It wears the logo of the Murray Valley Meat Trading Company, a red cow stood against a disc of yellow sun. Beneath this runs the words: A DIVISION OF WOODWARD INTEGRATED AGRIBUSINESS.

Upon the sixteenth clause authorising the assessment of one halfpenny on sheep, one penny halfpenny on cattle, and three pence on horses, half-yearly, being read, Mr. BERRY said, that with all due deference to the members of the sub-committee, he thought they had shaved too close, and that the sum they would be able to raise would be insufficient for the purposes contemplated.

In 2019, Woodward Foods sold a 49% minority ownership stake to Hairun Food Investment Holdings, a Hong Kong-based cold storage and logistics company, in order to expand its export of red meat to China.

Besides the loss to the consumer here is there not another element in this matter of waste to be considered—our export trade; do we not almost lose our export trade through the quality of meat we are able to send away?

cattle / *noun.*

[from Anglo-Norman, Old Northern French *catel*, from
Medieval Latin *capitale* 'property, stock']

Photographs of feedlots for cattle held prior to slaughter in
Queensland and Victoria show dead cows lying in the churn
of their faeces.

Each allotment of land, for which a Licence is thus given, is called a
Station, wrote Governor George Gipps to Lord John Russell, in
1840, after the passing of the Border Police Act, *and the Stations*
may vary in extent from 5,000 to 30,000 acres.

The persons, who form these Stations, are the real discoverers of
the Country, and they may be said to be in Australia (what the
Backwoodsmen are in America) the Pioneers of Civilisation.

Before I left for America, I had a letter **A**, the size of thumbprint, tattooed to the inside of my left forearm. The shape of it is based on an early Greek *alpha*, adapted in turn from the Phoenician *aleph*.

In Phoenician script, which emerged in lands now known as Syria, Lebanon and Turkey, the *aleph* was a representation of the head of an ox in profile:

Rotated 90 degrees, over centuries, the *aleph* would become the Greek *alpha*, then the Latin letter **A**.

cattle / *noun.*
[from Medieval Latin *capitale* 'property, stock', noun use of neuter of Latin adjective *capitalis* 'principal, chief', literally 'of the head', from *caput*, 'head'. Compare development of **fee, pecuniary**.]

Eleven days before you died, SIEV 221 ran aground on rocks just off the shore of Christmas Island. Forty-two people survived. Forty-eight people were drowned. The then Opposition Immigration Minister, Scott Morrison, suggested that the cost of funerals should not be borne by the Australian government.

It was the day after Christmas when you died. A flash of tinsel can still pull me back inside that summer's strange tonal saturation. I got sunburnt at your funeral; I thought I saw you sitting in the distance at your funeral.

That people who are not residents of this country, ————— ————————————————————————————————— ————————————————————— now we've got to pay ——— —————————————————————————————————— ————————

————————————————— grip on taxpayer's money ————————— ————————————— And it's wrong, isn't it? Isn't it wrong?

And our secret was the all-of-us together in the two of us, always. We wanted that always.

How do I say.

That I write this for us to assemble.

Which must sound naive.

When I say it that way.

Other versions of us have existed and will again, in time.

In 1852 there was a shortage of labour to build the Glebe Island abattoir, thanks to the rush on the goldfields in the colonies of New South Wales and Victoria.

[S]ince our arrival, wrote miners in 1857, who had travelled to these goldfields from China, *we have been subjected to a series of insults and oppressions from the ignorant, the cruel, and the malicious, though we are not conscious of having merited such injustice.*

In reaction to the racist violence—the most notorious incident of which, the 1861 Lambing Flat Riot, saw a mob of thousands of white miners assault Chinese miners, loot their possessions, and drive them from the Burrangong goldfields— the government of the New South Wales colony passed the Chinese Immigration Act in November 1861, a precursor to the White Australia Policy.

The Act prevented the naturalisation of Chinese migrants in the colony, and restricted their arrival by ship to *the proportion of one to every ten tons of the tonnage of such vessel.*

Somewhere, at the edge of what will pass into recorded history, a family memory, recalled to me, of labour strikes against the containerisation of the Sydney Harbour docks during the 1960s.

ALI DARYAB: I have been working for more than one year in, at the abattoir, Burrangong Meat Company, and all of the Young people are very friendly to me. I like to be in Young. But my visa runs for another 18 months and I didn't know about my situation after 18 months, what will happen with me. I'm worry about that. Yes, I'm worried.

TANYA NOLAN: Ali is one of up to ninety Afghan asylum seekers who's made a new life in the town of Young, after living in detention in Western Australia, and who is now fighting to maintain it.

Glebe Island abattoir was shuttered around 1913, when Sydney's main slaughtering facilities were moved further west, to the suburb of Homebush. During the Second World War, the site became a US Army base, then a concrete storage facility.

Increasing moves to containerisation of cargoes, which are now mostly handled at Port Botany, enabled a series of wharf closures in Sydney Harbour.

Marc changed his mind about the war.

The space between life and death is a state of exception in which there is much to fear, he wrote, from Verdun, *and much suffering.*

Within a week of the First World War beginning, all Germans living in Australia were classified as enemy aliens. Thousands were imprisoned, without trial, in detention camps, and, in 1915, the status of enemy alien was extended to include the Australian-born children of German and Austrian migrants. In 1919, the majority of these detainees were deported from Australia.

When I returned to the flat where I lived / on the lands of the Lenape six weeks after your death, my visa stamped, my thesis incomplete, opposite the freight dock, blaming poetry for the fact that no words could traverse this, I dreamt of you; or perhaps you dreamt me dreaming you and held us there? Sometimes I sense there is only a membrane between us.

Above my desk I keep a black-and-white photograph I took after you died, looking out of a window to the grounds of what had been our art school, which is now no longer an art school.

To the inside of the window, facing in towards a person looking out, I stuck a small photograph of a billboard we remade, to make a window of a photograph inside the window pane, the whole of it framed by this photo I keep above my desk: itself a window on a past that will have happened.

I believe another world is possible.

You noticed it first: the blank billboard on the road heading down towards the silos, near the art school that had been the asylum. This billboard was still lit up at night, an empty screen, an unexposed piece of photographic paper, long side of a container, no flag of any nation.

The thing to make was shadows, we decided; a mark but not a mark. Writing in light before photography existed. Before alphabets.

We found some empty oil tins and our hands grew slippery as we cut the tins with snips into the shape of flying birds, five shapes to cast the shadow of the idea of flight onto the billboard.

Then we climbed a ladder from the street to a roof, and a second ladder up to the billboard, and spent a while up there, adjusting wires that we'd brought to stay the shapes in their place in front of the footlights, our shadows cast too and intermingled with the animals.

Your partner photographed us from the street, and these are among the only photographs in which the two of us appear: dressed in hi-vis orange vests and pretending to be working.

Our work.

so partner, you write to me.

Do I think that art can change the world? No and yes. We can't end work—or war—with pencils, or by arguing for better television shows. But there are no movements towards freedom without what must be imagined, and perhaps can only be imagined: I believe that. Another way to put this would be to say that I believe in all of us because of all who have imagined this in the act of remaking a street or a room through some gesture of their hands, by writing or painting or playing, no matter how tentative the gesture or how ephemeral the evidence. We've got to play ordinary venues at the moment but I dream of playing the rubble of London's palaces.

I search the internet for clips of Tammi Terrell, and find one of her and Marvin Gaye lip-syncing to 'Ain't No Mountain High Enough'. It's VHS yellow, the footage, and the sound is scratchy, but I watch her, repeatedly, having fun with having to pretend. Pulling faces, little dances. Her workplace sabotage.

My love is alive, she mouths,
way down in my heart,
although we are miles apart,

and it makes me smile because, as she pretends to sing this, she's practically standing in Marvin's ear. She recasts the song as a game between the two of them.

I'm aloud

I'm aloud to go

In my dream we cannot speak, and we know we cannot speak, because language has ceased in this afterplace. We know that I'm alive and you are not. We do not break eye contact as we walk, hand in hand, in what I could describe as silence but is not.

An alternative to speaking. You lead me to your photographs and drawings, or to ours become yours in what your death has taken with you, which is us, among the living, in time. Other versions of us have existed, in time, where you would trace over my lines, or we could write our sentences together. Now we're holding on across the gap where language meets the edge of your materiality, your absence in the world. And we had fallen

together in our separateness, falling through a space that made us possible. We never break our gaze.

I have been waving to you through the window.

Georges Franju's documentary *Le Sang des Bêtes* begins with a still shot of a sculpture of a bull.

A still of a stillness, over which the credits then appear, in a series of fades:

Musique
Joseph Kosma

Commentaire
Jean Painlevé

Scénario et Réalisation
Georges Franju

In the still shot of the sculpture of the bull is the promise of an animal in motion, a model of motion: front leg, left, bent ahead of the right.

For the image in cinema (and not only in cinema), *is no longer something immobile. It is not an archetype, but nor is it something outside history: rather, it is a cut which itself is mobile,*

The border is a cut which is itself
mobile.

Dear Alya,

The property relations embedded in language—or, more correctly, in systems of writing—require a return to the beginnings of refusal to be ruled. To overturn these records of enclosures, we must keep moving, mourning, making, joining. Scatter, assemble. The border works to constitute us all, and I know that beyond the city's gates is not beyond the city's meaning. What days can we make for us free of the borders, except for the border between you and me.

Who might we be.

The Adelaide Advertiser, 30 March 2002

DETAINEES escaped after mingling with protesters who stormed the Woomera Detention Centre last night, tearing down a razor-wire perimeter fence.

In extraordinary scenes, more than 500 people ran the gauntlet of federal officers, with some running into the detention centre.

Several detainees—including children—were recaptured during numerous violent scuffles with South Australian police who finally intervened during the breakout.

It is believed some may still be free.

One woman detainee, walking from the compound to the protesters' camp with her young son, told *The Advertiser*: 'We just want our freedom.'

Among the Germans (or suspected Germans) deported from Australia after the First World War was Paul Freeman, a miner, and a member of the Industrial Workers of the World, aka the Wobblies.

In their paper *Direct Action*, which was printed in Australia between 1914 and 1917, the Wobblies wrote:

> The arrival in this country every year, of thousands of immigrants, is thought by the average wage-slave to be the cause of unemployment, but they forget that this curse is world-wide, and that these workers themselves have been forced to leave the land of their birth by the unemployment existing there... The real cause of unemployment is because the workers have not reduced the hours of their labour in proportion to the productivity of the machine.

And bats in the glory of their fruit trees,
and water
returned to the glaciers,
if we had asked better questions, if the picket

had been stronger; if we
are, if we

are to be

everything
will be extinguished,
unless

But outside of our appointed confrontations with a fraction of
the ruling class, we had no strategy: not in the workplace, or at
the distribution points of trade, where capital is vulnerable, to last

And then people were jumping from

the fence   and over

                                    the cops

had appeared,

                    and we all

                            had to run, and

            in doing so,   blend

                    shouts screams no
                    whistles people
                    sharing
                    their names.

Police Station,
Cloncurry,
Jan 11th, 1919.

Mr. James Hogan,
Curidala,

Dear Jim: —

Was arrested for deportation at 11 P.M., 8th Jan., in my camp, brought to Cloncurry and tomorrow morning will be taken direct to Brisbane from where they will most likely send me to the U.S.A.

In view of the above I would be very much obliged if you'd send three pounds eight shillings due me to George Cook who will forward the money to me in due time. Am constrained to confess of being unusually short of cash, which I will sorely need.

Please convey my best regards to Miss Hogan.

Regret my inability of bidding you good by personally but I suppose it can't be helped.

Wishing you all that is best in this world and hoping of corresponding with you sometimes in future,

I am,

Yours for The Revolution,
Paul Freeman.

If I invoke the ghosts of redressers past / it is because / I find myself afflicted by the sadness of thinking / it is too late to remember / now the future / and not wanting to surrender / to believing this

evenings, the carlight,   myself
                            inside a loop
                            of ghosts: each revolution
apparitional.

The earliest salt prints have ceased to exist, as they were made before a method to fix the image after exposure had been found.

Le Sang des Bêtes is on the internet now, which makes it harder to explain its hold on me; its living power in my memory diluted by the artefact.

I couldn't take it in—I mean the fact of the boat going down when I still had to hope that you would live.

And I know you would want me to say this:

They seem to have a grip on taxpayer's money ——————
———————————————————————————

that no death occurs in isolation from events that make some deaths count, while some are only counted. Or not counted.

The white horse is a distinguishable casualty; what follows is a dozen veal calves, a herd of sheep. Each animal's death is brought about by increments:

————————————————————————————

—————————— And it's wrong, isn't it? Isn't it wrong?

no one alone can say I am responsible.

And I had forgotten that what comes between the sculpture of the bull and the bolt gun is a context: pedestrians, children playing games of ring-a-rosy, a gramophone horn and radios stacked on a flea market table, at the gates of Paris.

We were the last students of photography to learn everything by analogue means, and the paper stocks and films were disappearing.

I'm standing on Pitt Street (you are dead by then): there's a snap protest in solidarity with asylum seekers being held on Manus Island, and the cops kettle us, so we sit in the middle of the shopping mall. I'm speaking with a young man and learn he's never heard of *Tampa*; it occurs to me that twenty years of detail has dissolved, and it gets harder to recall, in the absence of collective memory, how we arrived here: that none of this was ineluctable.

Time before, and time before, and who is being here, before

After your death someone called me to talk about you and I just couldn't remember them at all.

and always, and what gets done, and what is done. How does the settler declare her allegiance to no borders on the countries that will never be her own?

Ring back if you can hear me calling through the window.

At your grave, in those first weeks, I tried to concentrate my mind on the fact of your being there, the distance between us only feet.

ses sabots deviendront des engrais,

We built the fence / on Wangal country inside the gallery because we both had been to the desert. You drove across the Nullarbor. I went to a protest outside the Woomera Detention Centre / on Kokatha country.

The site of our art school is no longer an art school; I wonder if the disused buildings we broke into there are still piled up with gurneys, and whether old instructions still moulder on the walls, like the one we photographed that read: ALL PATIENTS FOOD MUST BE CUT INTO TINY PIECES.

Latent within the word *asylum* is the notion of something inviolable, without right of seizure.

In the interview room, when I lifted my sweater, the admitting doctor winced at the razor wounds across my torso.

Access to television is restricted and articles critical of detention centres are snipped out of newspapers. The government denies this.

The admitting doctor said to me: *You'll probably be in and out of places like this your whole life.*

In 1999, just after it had opened—with projected annual revenue of $14 million for the Wackenhut Corporation—six asylum seekers dug beneath the inner fence of Woomera Detention Centre and escaped.

Not that the internet remembers, in itself: it's an incomplete repository, which happens to be watching what we're watching.

Yesterday you put on shoes and socks, and so did many other people. But then, you do that every day. So maybe that's not very important. You may not even remember doing it yesterday.

Among the places we climb into in what was the asylum is a room with one chair in it, facing a mirror. You photograph yourself in the mirror, your single lens reflex camera held in front of your face, so that the damaged print I keep, its emulsion peeling, and the plaster lifting inside the room in the photograph, is part of a reflection of the sense I have that evidence—your face—is part-hidden but perceptible, a mirror moving in and out of the light's path, the trace of things both near to me and very far away.

                                                                Well,
history is like that.

Word got around the camp, on the first day, that people locked inside had asked to see our faces, so we walked the kilometre or so from our tents to the outer fence of the detention centre.

I remember a chain-link fence topped with barbed wire; I remember it unanchored, at both ends: an arbitrary line in the desert. But can that be right?

Evenings, the carlight, a sense there isn't time enough.

Weapons testing at Woomera was first conducted under the management of the Anglo-Australian Project, a joint defence project of the British and Australian governments, which was established in 1946, following Germany's deployment of long-range missiles during the Second World War.

Modern, Mature, Powerful, boasts the Raytheon website, of the *Tomahawk missile*, which has been used in bombings of Yemen and Syria.

I assume that when I search the internet for things like *Tomahawk missile*, some machine somewhere is keeping a record.

On 15 February 2003 roughly fifteen million people worldwide marched against the invasion of Iraq. The invasion began thirty-three days later.

A thousand people leant upon the outer fence and it began to sag beneath our weight;

I felt a kind of craziness that nothing could be done to stop the war. I felt that we were living in a box the ruling class could peer inside but from which no report leaked out.

what felt strange is that no one stopped us, or even tried to: the cops were notable in their absence.

When you think of what happened to you yesterday, as well as to all the other people in the world, that is history.

This sow died in the farrowing crate; her body has been rotting on the concrete for days. I believe that other animals than us wish to live and when we turn them into surplus made to die—we have been turning them—we wrong against the equilibrium of everything.

What felt strange is that no one stopped us, or tried to.

To repeat something is to make it possible anew.

The decision fell through us: to pull the fence down.

Here lies the proximity of repetition and memory.

A National Archives record search for the Anglo–Australian Project, returns, among other things, a listing for a series of *approximately 4,800 colour and black-and-white slides*, shot on 35 mm film, taken between 1948 and 1951. Along with aerial photographs of several parts of South Australia, the slides include *aboriginal cave paintings, sacred homes, native dress, carvings, Bushmen, children, dingoes and wildflowers* [sic].

Controlling records for this series indicate that, in total, 6,220 slides were registered between 1947 and 1971. The whereabouts of the missing slides is currently unknown.

And sometimes I chase the edges of your presence upon waking.

So farewell, I'm happy that you're working, wrote August Macke to Franz Marc in 1910, shortly after they had met. *Give to your age images of animals that people will stand and look at for a long time.*

Friendly fire, wrote Franz Marc to Maria Marc, of the French artillery that killed August Macke. Both men had learnt so much about the use of colour from their French peers.

Above my desk I keep a colour postcard reproduction of a sketch by Sonia Delaunay, *Sans Titres*: hemispheres and circles;

Form a circle: it takes less people that way to block a space than it would to block the same with a straight line.

I remember a line of flares arcing red against the sky,

A water cannon, shiny as a new toy,

A woman stood against the inside fence, and she said: *We are not animals. We are not animals.*

The noise increased as we got closer to the inside fence, running now across the sudden space we'd made by having pulled the outer fence down:

shouts, whistles, and then people

were jumping from the inside

fence and

---

over,   the cops

had appeared,
and the threshold

moving again
us moving
again moving

against the violence of the state.

There is no parity in mourning; there is no innocence that I could claim as distance from the border.

I watched a man ——————— razor wire ——————————
FREEDOM across his ———————————

The struggle against borders on a country not my own.

Or maybe ——————— FREEDOM ——————— using a broken-off

Whatever this might be.

Or becoming *we*.

Dear brother, my sister:

I am haunted by these minutes ever since:
what we do

        what do we do?

        when we bring the fences down:

a return
to the beginnings

of refusal
to be ruled,   but only on the grounds

        that nothing is unoccupied;

        no land
        no document
        unmade by precedent

before
the settler
world   is possible.

An elder came to talk to the protest camp, on the morning after the breakout. They were angry. Vulnerable people were now possibly at large and at risk on Kokatha country.

We had acted without thinking of this; we had acted as if this place were ours to act upon.

In reply, we (*we?*) could only describe the spontaneity of the escape: the force of will on both sides of the fences.

I had thought that we had done the right thing—in those moments, no other thing felt human—all of us, on both sides of the fences.

Pickets had developed in the camp, around the tents, to stop the people who'd escaped from getting picked off by the cops.

The threshold moving again.

But not even a stone here should be shifted thoughtlessly.

The talk was hard, around the campfire, with hundreds of us gathered, Aboriginal and non-Aboriginal. A history lodged between you and me. And I don't know that I would act differently in another time, or on another people's country,

so how does the settler betray

herself.

If his film had been in colour, said Franju, it would have been unbearable.

I always thought that if a person could imagine a blue horse, then it meant a kind of freedom;

FREEDOM?

we?

Who might *we* be?

We find some empty oil tins and our hands grow slippery as we cut them up with snips into the shape of flying birds—five aspects of a bird as it moves within the sky.

After you died I feared your voice would fade away from me. I would move beyond the shadow of your broadcast.

Here in this new grass,

This aftermath,

Somebody said to me: *You'll find him again, keep switching through the dial.*

Years later / on Gadigal country, I watch a documentary by Patricio Guzmán, *The Cordillera of Dreams*, in which he reflects upon the legacy of the coup against Salvador Allende in 1973, which he and his friends documented.

I think about the fact that the landmass now known as Chile was attached to the landmass now known as Australia, a hundred million years ago.

For my unforgettable Franz Marc / THE BLUE RIDER / till the end of time, wrote Else Lasker-Schüler in the dedication to her anti-war novel *Der Malik*, in which she continued with her letters to Marc, though he was dead.

The small rope of dreaming / the future I remember;

Guzmán says: *This film is a reflection of a past that is pursuing me.*

seriously what about our plan to take over the world.

History is ours, and people make history.

don't think I've forgotten about it.

Guzmán says that those who sided with the coup understand this history *in a fascist way*, as epic and mythological.

What happened to you yesterday, as well as to all the other people in the world: that is history.

But what happened was ordinary, banal and heinous.

We simply cannot allow ————————————————
————————————————————————————

————————————————————————————
———————————————— as a country ————————————

We don't turn ————————————————

irrespective of the circumstances ————————————
————————————————————————

And everything is possible and will remain so in the space that has created you and me.

Nothing living can make me less culpable.

Still I believe I must stumble towards we.

A man leads a horse to the gates of an abattoir.

The horse and the man stand together in the courtyard of the abattoir.

A streak of lilac divides two yellow hills in Franz Marc's painting
Pferd in Landschaft.

I stay with the painting for a long time, as if the horse inside it
could transport me

to you, animal

        and breathing, as if you are

the lilac shade of the foxgloves I laid on the Marcs' grave.
I twisted them out of the gravel by the churchyard,
St Michael's, Kochel-am-see.

In the gallery, a sheet of paper rested on her knees,
a child is drawing the horse,

remaking the world. I have finished
our work now.

The horse is pansy purple with a sapphire mane.
The hills are underlain by green,
and shade at the crests into goldenrod.

Clouds mauve across the sun, and the variable light

falling

       through a frosted door near where the painting is hung

changes it
bright,   dark,

bright:
you had
red hair,   brown eyes.

       Sometimes I sense
       there is only a membrane
       between us.

Sometimes I hear you in the light.

for Ned Sevil

(1980–2010)

If you take a sheet of paper and place it in front of the lens, you will see clearly on the paper all that goes on outside the house. This you will see most distinctly at a certain distance, which you will find by moving the paper nearer to or farther away from the lens, until you have found the proper position.

Daniele Barbara, 1568, *La Practica della perspettiva*

The opening epigraph is taken from Fanny Howe's *The Winter Sun: Notes on a Vocation*, Graywolf Press, Minneapolis, 2009. The closing epitaph is quoted in Helmut and Alison Gernsheim's *The History of Photography: from the Earliest Use of the Camera Obscura in the Eleventh Century Up to 1914*, Oxford University Press, Oxford, 2007.

This work includes appropriations from a range of sources, including but not limited to: newspaper articles, radio transcripts, children's reference books and technical manuals on photography.

The development of this work has been supported by the Copyright Agency, the University of Technology Sydney, and Varuna, the National Writers' House.

Composed between May 2017 and February 2020. Revised between June and October 2020. An early extract of this work appeared in *The White Review*, Issue 26, October 2019.

PO Box 4
Enmore NSW 2042
Australia

ANWEN CRAWFORD is a Sydney-based writer, critic and visual artist. Her essays have appeared in publications including *The New Yorker*, *The White Review*, *Frieze*, *The Monthly*, *Best Australian Essays*, *Meanjin*, *Overland* and *Sydney Review of Books*. In 2021 she won the Pascall Prize for Arts Criticism. Her book *Live Through This* (2015), on the Hole album of the same name, is published by Bloomsbury in the 33⅓ series, and was named by *Pitchfork* as one of the '33 best 33⅓s'. She is a graduate of Sydney College of the Arts, where she studied photography, and of the School of the Arts, Columbia University, where she completed a Master of Fine Arts in poetry.

Transit Books is a nonprofit publisher of international and American literature, based in Oakland, California. Founded in 2015, Transit Books is committed to the discovery and promotion of enduring works that carry readers across borders and communities. Visit us online to learn more about our forthcoming titles, events, and opportunities to support our mission.

TRANSITBOOKS.ORG